"How to Pull Apart the Earth is a kaleidoscope of perspective and narrative, providing genuine connection between images and people that are simultaneously adjacent and worlds apart. This conveys that our world is not just ours, we share it, as Cordero so generously conveys in her poems. The transformative quality of her work, 'in my hands i hold the skull of a wolf. i wake & in my palms a honey crisp apple,' gives to us the elusive nature of reality, how memory and nationality merge into selfhood, how selfhood is begotten of lineage, how lineage is derailed by colonialism, how colonialism is, 'rooted & hungry. hungry for sun & sun too will be hungry.' This book is on time and in time."

—**Aziza Barnes**, Author of *i be, but i ain't*

"Karla Cordero is a poet who knows that words can dance, even over an earth as distressed as ours. Here is a stunning collection of sweet things gone sour, of ghosts and borders, chopping blocks and the hands that haunt them. These poems are full of patience, and full of fire."

—**Bao Phi**, Author of *Thousand Star Hotel*

"In *How to Pull Apart the Earth*, Cordero turns the border into a sleeping mother, a raindrop into the Pacific, a turtle shell into a home. She introduces magical realism into her poetry effortlessly, evoking images many of us have forgotten to revisit in a long time. This magnificent piece of work is a litany to the miracle of migrant generations preserving their magic, each word is a rosary bead, a seed, a blissful garden amongst drought."

—**Yesika Salgado**, Author of *Corazón*

"The poems in *How to Pull Apart the Earth* are rooted in a strong sense of place and are informed not just by the hardship of living and being raised in the borderland, but also by the joy that is found there. These poems seek to understand how the familial and historical past has shaped the fraught present and in turn how the present will shape the unknowable future. This collection of poems is a lush garden in the desert—a space where it is said nothing can grow, but when tended to by skilled hands, like Cordero's, persists to bloom, and yields a bounty in imagining."

—**Alfredo Aguilar**, Author of *What Happens On Earth*

HOW TO PULL APART THE EARTH

poems

KARLA CORDERO

Cordero, Karla

ISBN: 978-1-945649-25-7

Edited by Safia Elhillo
Cover art and design by Juan Charlie Beaz
Cover design by Mario DeMatteo
Editorial design by Ian DeLucca
Proofread by Rhiannon McGavin

Printed in Canada

Not a Cult
Los Angeles, CA

For Petra con luz y amor

For my Mother, Father & Familia Cordero

In Memory of Alfonso 'Buelo' Cordero

"Our love was born
outside the walls,
in the wind,
in the night,
in the earth,
and that's why the clay
and the flower,
the mud and the roots
know your name."

—Pablo Neruda

*"But it's no use now, thought poor Alice, to pretend to be two people!
Why, there's hardly enough of me left to make one respectable person!"*

—Alice In Wonderland, Lewis Carroll

CONTENTS

i

ii

iii

iv

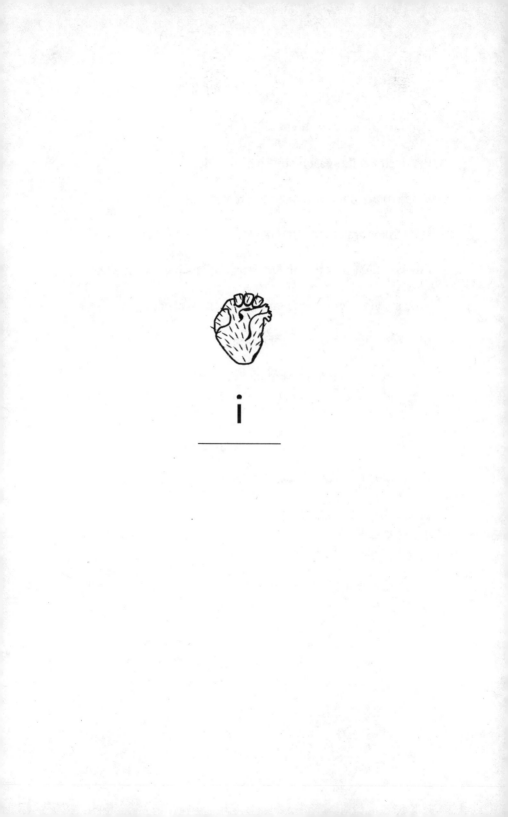

i

BORN AT THE CIRCUS

i don't believe quiet to be a good song.

i know this. how my body whispered into light

the doctor calling each bone a still child

& i go on & on to recreate my creation story.

start from scratch. toss the noiseless pieces of bone

down a flight of stairs. the marrow collapsing a yellowness.

now a yellow tent. the tongue unfolds a wet carpet.

the accent marks un-tame the lion.

the spanish the lion who circles the stadium.

all the seats filled by the strumming notes of uvula

waiting for the grand finale. the wild cat in

all its rolled r's never jumps through

hoops lit by fire. but is the fire. free & feral.

an unstoppable snarl.

I'M ASKED ABOUT HOME

& contemplate the space between mattress & roof.
       the ceiling claimed not to be a house.

i mistook a kitchen for warm hands— found shelter
       inside my mother's fingerprint. saw her eyes play

in the dirt. she slept on top of buildings
       when rain announced itself— collected water

for thirst & hot rice. my father's tired skin
       became a photo album & i see a brown boy

harvest an apricot—he dreams under
       a tree with his family for a summer.

my feet know home when the mouth
       says: *right here for now.* the clothes on my back

carry the sun's beat down. i save corn husk
       in my pocket. waltz in an acre of dry grass.

BISABUELA MARRIED A SPANIARD

twenty years older than her palms   & my hands slice   the necks
of marigolds   offer their afro-petal heads to ask   did sun between
corn husk bathe in the warmth   of your cheek first   did he
offer leather   the dead deer shot   by the   vile bullet
offer red meat   what part of my bones belong   to the ship
          that broke the sea   that broke your tongue
did he lace every birthed child   in silver   spoon   fed
a language unknown   to half the blood they own   choked
on each letter   i give these thoughts many names: clipped
wings
                    wind   as myth
                                the acrobat who lives in this flesh

WHERE I INHERET MY SILENCE

i once walked into
my grandfather's shadow

dug for spanish
with a stick of dynamite

felt it explode
on my mother tongue

i bruised
& he called them flowers

i spoke english
& he fed me more spanish

until my stomach knew
the taste of vinegar

how his gold ring whistled
me to sit & stay

& i became
a puddle of mud

i split myself in half
like any good exorcist

accent marks left me
like a startled bird

& i have yet
to speak honey

i carry pieces
of a tambourine

still searching
how to be a choir

NOPAL EN EL FRENTE

cactus forehead is what they call the kids
with broken spanish. by high school

i grew a cacti tower fifty miles high between
cloud lovers beyond the blushing of horizons

where mother moon strings a line from branches
& dries her laundry after the wash.

spines puncture the sky prick the black vultures angry.
abuela says spanish belongs in my blood lives fluent

in the soft of my gums. she blesses each needle with her frail
palms: *en el nombre del padre, el hijo, y el espirito santo.*

HISTORY OF WALLS

our home has a fence the color of dead blood.
once my sister launched her barbie into the neighbor's yard
& in flight the small body stares back knowing it wouldn't
return or at least not the same. the next two days
the sky poured out all its water. a plastic girl goes missing
& a wet tombstone is born.

my hometown rhymes with mexico & ends with a wall.
a vertical ladder built all wrong & lays on its side like a sleeping
mother forgetting to feed her legacy. the children don't know
how to wake her. their bellies wail. mouths wide open.
their tongues a sea of small pink hands reaching for the sky.

DRIVING DOWN HIGHWAY 111

my nose bitters to cow manure

    as lettuce fields pass the car window

like green snakes with straight spines

    & men who dare play with such growth

knife & box the leaves

    behind their sweat-licked bandanas

they speak about their wives'

    humble teeth or predict

how full their cast-iron pots wait at home

    swollen in broth-boiled rice & cilantro

they gossip about the wall

    that one day will redefine the number

of torn children it takes to get

    to the center of a grieving mother

to understand the new purpose

    for bending metal & nail

HIS JAWBONE CAGED MY GRANDFATHER'S SKIN

For Alfonso Cordero

the same skin on braved bone/ once picked
apricots on an orchard farm/ like delicate
newborns/ such sweet children he had/ during
the humid summers/ he slept in the shade/ of
any tree/ praying to the moon/ or stars/ or
god/ across the sky/ like silver dollars far
from his reach/ how beautiful he dreamt/ that
night of a home/ built of sore knee/ tired
back/ when the orange man found a place in
america/ some cheered/ others cried their
body funeral/ but what does crying mean in
this country/ my abuelo sits at the kitchen
table/ fox news spills into the same air/ he
labors to belong in/ his resistance:/ swatting
the fruit flies/ over a browned apple

WATCHING THE GREEN MILE FOR THE FIRST TIME & I DREAM THAT NIGHT KNOWING JOHN COFFEY COULD HAVE ALSO BEEN MY FATHER

the moon's glare stitches a nightmare
to the wet of my eyes. i envy the violence of time—

how the clock hammers through seconds
& the room unfolds itself—

beige walls. boxspring. tired mattress.
i see my father now in the desert under a mesquite.

his lips signed by the sun. *drink.*
hands me a mason jar & water fogs

beneath a rusted lid. our footsteps close to home
far from god. a lizard on a piece of petrified wood

swallows my passport & grins.
father stares down my frail body & inhales

the fear out my eyes & an exhale of canaries
flood the sky. they sing heavy rain

& disintegrate into the clouds.
a wolf leaps down a cliff

& devours the last yellow bird to brush
the horizon. all the fear in his belly—

i hear it peck at the dark. tunes a sorrowful
prayer— a call to my father.

in my hands i hold the skull of a wolf.
i wake & in my palms a honey crisp apple.

ARRIVAL

petra arrived by bus

       & a north star's pointed finger

& before that by fake papeles

       & a smuggled plane ride

& before that by mud-covered knees

       a bouquet of blue flowers buried in her thighs

& before that from nayarit— from el rancho

       the womb to five children

       now she's momma's backbone

    my first secret
    my scraped elbow curandera
    my swap meet chingona
    my caldo bruja
    my brown heart hermana
    my understanding del otro lado
    my otro lado

I WATCH ALL THE DROUGHT THE DESERT CARRIES

& swallow a bottle of water & i am nourished by a captured current & this body's civilization prospers. momma would say: irrigate the throat & a garden blossoms & i remember petra. how she once traveled through tumbleweed. from mexico to a land that promised her heavy pockets. she'd find refuge under cacti & lick clean the tops of shade-covered stones. prayed for angry clouds & on the third day the sky offered pieces of the pacific & a woman's hands become a canteen. her lips the edge of a glass holding another day of breath & in all its pouring a vision of children who'd carry her name. how her body carries the blood of those who are thirsty. forced to uproot a mouth & grow a tongue without the taste of a past. where one day her children will float on a river. skip rocks the size of black beetles & tell stories of how their mother was made of dust. how the same dust grew into an endless storm.

EVERYTHING DIES HERE

this city dries every mouth
a land where sun owns

our bodies. men continue to harvest
onion—pant like street dogs for pennies.

their wives count babies—include the chickens.
slam tortillas flat & stir soup pots for hours.

the children learn to move slow for preservation.
draw crayon glaciers then lick the paper soggy.

mother this desert murders me slow—

i crave rain—let me run kite string
on arid fingers & leave this city.

search out meadows & learn the taste
of morning dew.

IN PRAISE OF SNOW

my sister cuts construction paper
snowflakes. tacks each piece of artificial

winter on cactus petals. she ignores
rebellious needles. brushes them off & claims

a december frost in our backyard. over adobe walls
lizards salivate as ice cubes between our

lips tell stories under palm trees.
i tell her it's snowing outside

as our mother & tias gossip
ridiculing the neighbor's daughter

who sports snow boots—the chola who got
pregnant from a boy twice her age. they giggle

& blame the heat. i tell my sister to never
have children with a man who sweats too much.

i say drink plenty of water & avoid this city's
snowmelt where everything sticks & stays. we make

our promise over snow puddles. lay our backs to the cold
waving our arms & legs. we escape an avalanche snowing

our way. now bathed in ice—we smile. notice the ice angels
fossiled into the ground & open our eyes.

CHRISTMAS

palm leaves pluck the winter air & café de canela smack
our lips as the boom box howls frank sinatra's: *let it snow!*
i savor these miracles cuz today a child is born under
a bethlehem star & tomorrow he prepares to live among
them. in the kitchen mom swears the pozole's gettin' cold.
i whisper *impossible*. the gas stove kickin' the blue flame
& a boilin' pot becomes a prayer. sprouts legs & becomes
a pilgrimage to bless a home built by the brick of too
many stories ending with *la migra chased us & we made
it*. i think damn blessed. i think of ways to put a bow on all
this holy cuz outside on 2nd street cardboard is a mattress
made to trick bones to warmth yet teeth still chatter
& no one listens. guilt a song that calls to repair
the floorboards. a famished mouth. a bitter ghost.
& franky hits the high note: *oh the weather outside
is frightful!*   *let it snow! let it snow! let it snow!*

TENOCHTITLAN

tio goyo once knew a man who climbed
a mountain that wouldn't have him

& yet in the name of faith his feet scaled
rocks rusted like crooked knives—

& in his denim pocket he kept a polaroid
of a child with wind-pushed hair.

at the highest peak a star fed him
honeysuckles & he lost his appetite

for death. soon he clung to the sky.
his arms flashing feathers like gold.

he became a bronze-tailed eagle
slicing through clouds

above a sea of prickly pear cacti
who called themselves a banquet.

he floated down & devoured a serpent
to watch the sand below his beak

turn crimson. villagers drag
their feet & baskets full of infants

peeling back the dirt across their faces.
toes raving over the touch of fallen warmth.

ii

I ONCE CRACKED OPEN THE EARTH

& pleaded clay & rock to bear
children & over its bones without worm or root

acquired a father's shovel. kneaded life
into the dead. it wasn't easy.

each hand like blood-warm rakes welcomed new soil
& made a stubborn ground collapse into

small riverbeds but no river. i funeraled
each seed to rest. such tiny slices of moon or perhaps

a metaphor for womb & how the body can be a sky
to hold the stars. then the hose nozzle made a good rain

& grieving & motherhood were forgotten. watched
the sun keep the sunken warm. a tomb learning to be

a home. how children too outgrow their own safety
& sprout into the tallness of a cloud.

HIJA DE LA COSECHA

spoiled child of root. green leaf &
fruitful. child of mouthful-harvest.
mouth full of cherry tomato
blistering by the day's shower
of light. full on lemon juice made
to pucker. then sliced into
kindness by sugar cubes. here
vines run feral. the green-sheened
jalapeno trick an army of teeth to
burn. the birds tower the city on
top of sunflower faces. here
the carrots offer their silent bodies
& resurrect when mouths go
hungry. here i savor the wild
blueberry. swirl the sweetness
after each navy pebble pops
between teeth. *i remember* i was
once the child of broken earth.
mouth full on wind flavored by a
mother's *immigrant dream* coated
in lifeless rock. i crayoned the
seeds & stems of things i had yet
to savor. i was fed what was
given.

THE TIME MY MOMMA GAVE ME THE CHANCLA FOR LETTING ANDREW JACKSON ESCAPE OUT THE WINDOW

it is 12:00pm we arrive home from sunday church i am the last person to enter through the door & mom yells *cierra la puerta the AC is running* which means she just put in seventy hours of work this week to pay the bills which means to feel cold is a privilege a ghost visit thanks to mom's labor of love a desperation to put pan & milk on the table for her four daughters one time in the boiling summer of 1999 mom gave me the chancla for leaving the window open she swore she saw a flock of dollar bills fly out the window & soar through the sky the tip of each green wing printed with the number 20 & on their bellies an image of andrew jackson waving farewell & outside they flew & outside the sun burned each thin paper bird to a crisp before they could find freedom & claim it their own i still remember the bruise on my left butt cheek when i failed to foil the windows to keep the devil out & it was almost as hot then as it is right now but inside the house the house is breathing a cold breath how blessed to know the luxury of shiver to know the taste of snow in a place it does not exist

MOMMA KNOWS ALL THE MONSTERS'
HIDDEN TEETH

momma foresees mocos & gripa. she says: i dare you. bare your
feet on the tile floor & watch a glacier swallow your ankles into
sickness. go ahead. sleep wet-haired & watch water take nest onto
the pillow. watch it drown your throat into sickness. my momma
knows all the monsters' hidden teeth. she says: go on. befriend
the fire & the vela's wick will bite all the little fingers & make a
burning church of your body. when the moon demands closed eyes.
do so. el cucuy still thirsts. y ya sabes de la llorona. her trickery a
result of sadness. be a good girl. too many lonely mothers whose
children found in wind a loving embrace.

> then found mtv. & drogas. & sexo.

those poor mothers. who will they feed now.
> all that pan & leche gone to waste.
> > what a waste of pan & leche.

mija remember your mother & the vaporu.
> how they clung to your feet to save
> > you from ailment.

remember you are a floresita.
> rooted & hungry. hungry for sun
> > & sun too will be hungry.

I LEARNED TO TIPTOE FOR:

sidewalk spit-shined by icarus's curse/
heatstroke-grass inviting weeds to thorn
teeth/ black bristle welcome mat/
like a thousand dried spider legs/
fabuloso-touched-tile/ like ocean chasing
lavender fields across the kitchen floor/ &
momma says: let it dry/ no shadow-toes/
no tiny moon scars/ let the floor dry or *vas
a ver*/ at bath time bathwater blindfolds
the mirror/ see how a body finds a body/
inside a captured pond/ steaming bar of
soap—/ she says: scrub your feet /enforce
the walls of a house on fire/ she says:
limpieza is absolution/ in the scent of pine

IN A DREAM A SMALL STATUE
OF LA VIRGEN DE GUADALUPE
PREPARES TO DIVE FROM THE BOOKSHELF

the blue tile floor claims
    to be a salt-dipped sea

        as la virgen presses
        her hands together

    to baptize a body
    perhaps to hold the voices that call her

she removes a green veil
    each star unravels & returns to an empty sky

i caution &
she tells me:
        pull your eyes from the lightless room of doubt

    as a child i handed myself
      to a man-made pond

      & a father reached to return
        his daughter's lungs
    to the world

  buried in chlorine
    a throat filled with bad water

    i out-molded a child's frame
      & became anchor

you see she says asi es la vida & la virgen's feet let go

EL RANCHO 92'

i see a country in each eye
as her hand & comb rake my scalp.

loose strands far from her reach like méxico.
aqua net tightens my ponytail as she tells stories

of a place where milk is actually milk
& chickens bless the land in eggs & feather.

el rancho, she says, *is where the sun splits open the sky
to burn cornfields gold, to brush the onion leaves,*

& pigs carcass their way back to earth. i remember
my young tongue ask, when can the goats & chickens visit?

petra's black braid snakes across her back
the perfume of desert still caught in flesh

a mountain between here & motherhood—
never, she says, *they're busy feeding my children's bellies.*

TRUTHS AT THE ALL-AMERICAN CANAL

The canal has become sort of a national moat on our southern border, and
hundreds of people have perished in its waters. It is a carnage that has gone
mostly unnoticed because many of the victims are buried without their names
—*CBS News*

at the canal a child carries a penny in his palm/
pretends he stands/ in front of a fountain/
a naked deity/ spewing a waterfall/ back
to a blue stone glittered pool/ he tosses the coin
& begs it to shape-shift/ into a father's arms/
a mother's eyes witness a coin's surrender

a man slaughters a tree & gives birth
to a boat/ who learns to be the opposite
of a drowning/ who learns to break
water/ a kind of labor we have yet
to name/ but give a boat a beating heart/
& write sacrifice across its forehead/
carve ~~american~~ *dreamer* down to its bone

i watch the canal claw a tattered shirt/
bloated in its own ghost/ a thick neck/
sleeves filled with arms/ soaked in pigments
of gasoline & dust/ on the chest blood
stains dissolve/ & i too witness
how blood can be a homeless child

A LESSON IN SEWING

it's an art she whispers
to be patient for something
so small. petra shows me how to sew
how to hoop thread between needle—
i watch her patch my father's denim pants
as she watches me sew
a shirt for my stuffed bear.
i study how her fingers braid patience
i replicate the ritual & prick my index.
blood with patience stains the bear's belly.
petra laughs *es una flor*
like a flower rooted in dead-earth
with patience to bloom.

ABUELA IS A MACHETE WRAPPED IN HER FAVORITE APRON

a man once slammed a fruit bowl against the kitchen wall & abuela learned how glass can birth small daggers. she replaced her husband with knives. holds a blade like a loaded gun. enjoys the chop of cilantro-bundles for caldo & people swear she got lawnmowers for fingers. in the backyard the trees shed fruit baskets but abuela dislikes the rind. can scalp a pear's skin in seconds. clean. see the sugar bleed off the slice. each hand a steady butcher. never once nicked a thumb & for thirty years pierced meat. sliced basil. stripped salmon of its glittered gills. then dr. gonzalez found her memory carved to pieces. handed her plastic flatware. all her metal went dull. the good utensils for steak hidden. the house keys chained to her apron & sometimes her mouth switchblades when the keys go missing. today at the grocery store i tell her stories about the palms she owns. how they once tricked a carrot to dance like bright confetti & abuela picks a fresh pear. the heavy end cleansed by the fog of her mouth. she swears she's always loved the fruit's pale flesh & her teeth a wooden drawer of machetes.

A BROWN GIRL'S BLUES
After Natalie Diaz

there is a demon between my eyes
     a fanged beast/ a nightmare in shadowed veils
who rips root from bone/ some maniac killer of ancestry
       a cyclops stitching brown girl nicknames
el diablo dressed in america

there are wounded sparrows between my lips
     a choir in shackles/ broken beaks
& rusted tongues/ new scars behind feathered backs
      caged throats/ screaming for parrot color
 mocking a white kid's tune

there is a kitchen knife between my breasts
     a blacksmith dimple/ village of spears howling
to mother moon/ a razor lump/ shaman chants
      between hillsides/ blood on silver coin/ a wealth
so rich in earth/ men are hungry to settle their flags

there is a brushfire between my hips
     a savage dance/ matches shoved in sick children's bellies
cigarette torches & kerosene chimneys
      tumbleweed on candle wick/ lava ash & ghost cry
how dangerous to burn/ before the fall

there is a cemetery between my legs
     a war bleeding over riverbanks/ tombstones
for crippled grandmothers/ lost bodies in high grass
      sacred stone/ orchards swaying gentle
bullets/ mud/ cracked palms/ & prayer

ABUELA'S HAIR

abuela is losing
the photo album

in her brain.
but she knows

what clean hair
looks like.

i remind
her: *the salon at 3:00pm.*

at 3:00pm abuelo still
eats machismo & toast.

takes abuela to the casino.
her hair tangled

in cigarettes & penny slots.
she calls: *jackpot*

with empty picture frames
in her eyes.

God noticed how people
fondle madness so he
quarried stone whittled it down   to
a rib cage of bridges to cross
from spring to the edge and around
in order to seek a new way forward
the privilege of burgundy tells us
redemption runs without trouble on tongue
preserve the palette of burning
ballooning lungs expand   to
chandelier against dark
fruitful sleep

We cage ourselves with warmth
put wire around land
justify raking leave
unable to [pull] freedom home
we breathe mistake saving the greed
in brine behind the sternum forgiveness
cast the vessel for churning we pour out
an invite to dry out sin on our throats
taste sugar cane and tarmac...well done now
accordion muscle
jealous of gravity's
un relent

32

LEAKED AUDIO FROM A DETENTION CENTER

*On June 2018, audio from inside a U.S. Customs and Border Protection
Detention Facility captures undocumented children crying. Recorded audio
by an anonymous source was handed to Civil Right Attorney, Jennifer Harbury
and given to ProPublica for release.*

hear how the children   eat their tears

how the rain   in their throats   demands to be a river

yet their palms be: drought   dirt grave   dead fish

quiet rock   anchor rust   but know this:

grief can be   a kind of music   that knows how to rise

      like the sea

iii

DON'T BE AFRAID TO SPEAK:

if your language fractured its leg/ dislocated
a shoulder/ if its nose bled a river to the lips/
if its teeth don't dance/ if the tongue mops
floors/ if the mouth vagabonds spitting
cuentos/ watch ten fingers be ten people
finding their place in the world/ or room/ or
palm/ if language has a palm made of roads/
travel them all/ if the knee pop-locks too
tired/ if language punctured the heart/ be
the oxygen/ be the restless inhale/ be
the exhale for the language/ whose tattered
heart/ will beat for you

METAMORPHOSIS FOR SPEAKING SPANISH

under the bed you reach for a wooden box engraved

with your grandmother's throat—& inside crawls

a language eager to say *recuerdo*—

you reach in & grab a handful of insects

consume their giving bodies

hear them dance down your stomach

heavy as a mother's praying

hands & in that moment 27 wings

plummet off the entrails that wake

every cord

covered in cinder

a flood flickers in your mouth full of fireflies

they gather in the shape of a small tongue to

lead your teeth to song

all that sings departs

& all that spills

a frail beam of light

PARTS & DEFINITIONS FOR MESTIZA-MOUTH

mouth: jar of water thinks itself a river

lips: a cracked boulder beckons the wind

teeth: stained glass inside a charred cathedral

gums: dried cement scatters the echo of a rolled "r"

tongue: a pink scorpion's raised tail

palate: a wet cave in a language looking for a way out

CHICANA LEARNS SURVIVAL FROM THE TEENAGE MUTANT NINJA TURTLES

I am a turtle, wherever I go I carry 'home' on my back –Gloria Anzaldúa

1. when your middle school teacher grades you on your english.
   & your machismo of a grandfather tells you spanish is who you
   should be. speak turtle. embrace your voice's ability to break
   & bend. be the brave child who gives birth to: cowabunga
   tubular & radical. how radical it is to be a child with wild teeth for
   talking. find refuge in a language that sounds of home
   & *yes you belong.*

2. beg your parents for pizza in the morning. settle for a hot
   pocket. practice the art of full belly. full heart. leave no room for
   oppressor. face the villain when you become a victim of critical
   race theory. when the blonde woman at target asks you for
   a sweater in another size. riot in your belly. tell the bully disguised
   as shredder that her ignorance is another word for privilege.
   & become your own savior.

3. you will discover that green skin is as mutant as *what are you
   skin.* when asked "what are you" translates into *the world
   don't know our history be written by blood & bullet.* you will
   live underground not because you are hiding. but because you
   miss the soil that molded you mestiza mixed not messy. motherland
   not martyr. learn to understand the roots that make
   you complicated magic before this world labels you ghost.

4. when the foot clan kidnaps splinter the metaphor will finally
   make sense. history will visit. attempt to rob our tongues. silence
   our pain. learn to scream your body into a turtle shell. a mountain.
   a safe house. something strong. such unbreakable creatures we are
   to rebuild. to mold breath. to speak stone. taking to the streets—
   announcing the sequel to how we survived it all.

SAFE HOUSE

truth is

      mothers pray their whole lives
for steel babies

crafted by fire
& tender hands

      our fragile cries
brought by false light

how the first wind to kiss our necks

      does not caution
how the earth's bones are painted crimson

& we yearn to crawl on feeble knees

thirsty for milk
      then hunger to be present

& when every breath builds a bombed out city

you learn to be
      a safe house

      brick a furnace

spit the smoke
      & watch it speak vicious

THIS SKIN BE

born from wolf womb.
bowls of blood moon.

bone know crow sob.
know moss mouth.

know cop look.
know oak cross

blooms body into
ghost fog. cold box tomb.

fold. absolve.   *poof.*
now jukebox dove song.

howl home god. howl home.

ZOO OF EDEN

i wonder if god knew
a selfish beast

would arrive
to his garden

make a zoo
of everything colored.

when i was little
i used to look

through the fence
made of iron rod goliaths—

my dad would say:
the wall keeps

this land white.
says: *the statue of liberty*

would never travel
to mexico.

i see how my sneakers
step on the same soil

of those on the other side.
their hunger pushing

swollen bellies
against ribcage.

their blistered feet
their blood thick with light

how god's creatures
[almost] look human.

DEITY

the vast summer harvest blessed our
mouths. wild onion—its green leaves

like claws bathing in the blaze of day
tomato stems beasting a tallness no one

foresaw would bear such sweet
balloons of red sugar & nothing here

floats on its own. the branches knew this
& felt purposeful. dusk made itself known

& snails hovered taking the lives
grounded by root. peeled the sweet onion without

mercy. then took its neighbor & the children.
swallowed the cherry tomatoes—a broken

string of lights & no glow
remained & the branches lost purpose.

overcome by the smallest violence
i plucked each shell-holding-body.

rubber beings clinging to leaf & i plucked
with even more given strength. retreating into

the only home given to them by birth—a prison-weight
on their backs. still i felt nothing. lined one-by-one

across the faded wooden edge of the garden box.
a green village surrounding the guilty. i was both judge

& executioner. raised a brick & let go. their
brittle shells cracking. how my ears understood

the dead. their bodies taken by an evaporating
sky. the ruins of homes remain. but to hold life

then remove it from soil is to costume myself
a deity—a skin not my own & still i act with an itch—

how often i hear of war & the world itching in someone else's
skin—feeling nothing but a raised brick in their hands.

WHAT BECOMES OF WAR & NAME

today a man spoke power from his jaw
& said yes to tomahawk missiles
& the people of syria become tombstones.

i imagine a family whose name rips
into a thousand lost limbs
& smoldering marrow.

the smoke clouds the clouds & brittle bodies
listen for their mother's porcelain cry.
homes become firewood & streets

bitter the air with wet copper.
soldiers carry their guns like
cold crucifixes

forgetting the children under piles of stone
are still children. small hands rising from
the dust like blooming daisies thirsty

for a merciless sun.
i dig my spoon into a bowl of cheerios.
somewhere in syria a father digs for his son's body.

THE FIRST TIME I MET THE KKK

it was halloween of 99'— i was cat woman.

a ghetto michelle pfeiffer knock off. mexican girl.

skinny framed in soggy black spandex collecting

tootsie rolls & jawbreakers at every knocked door.

down the street bushes shaped like skyscrapers

a herd of older kids parade dressed in white robes

& white cone shaped masks. they talk about women's

asses cussing between sentences. their eyes

trace murder chalk around my body. i clutch the bag of candy

they see the stiffness hold my legs hostage

against catcall & echo. i dare walk past an army of ghosts.

everything in me regrets the black cloth pressed

against my pubescent figure. i turn & flip them a middle finger.

all the sheet-wearing bodies cloud into a huddle

& throw a lump of weight at my feet. they laugh—

& the bushes swallow their shadows.

i look down to see mr. bill's dead cat. all fur & fresh blood.

MY COUNTRY IS PANTING

my country is panting double
its normal weight—
stone-heavy

my country watches
its guilt—licks its paws clean
like a wounded dog—
& a boy's footprints are shot in the sand

my country
licks the cheek of a boy
they shot
& another boy they shot
& when they shot a third boy

my country
like a lost dog
slept

DINNER WITH CORNEL WEST

i wait for the boiling soup to settle. notice
how the vegetables swim together

steam an exiled ghost & the tv screams
about the new sewage flooding ferguson.

my tongue burns on broth in an uproar forgetting
the piece of squash escaping my spoon dives back

in the heap of its bowl. ferguson continues to fall.
voices protest. 49 arrests practicing the first amendment ·

& mr. cornel west pushes through the dirt of law.
he's too elegant for police siren & pepper spray dressed

all black suit tie & silk scarf. cornel must be hungry rustling
through the herds of uniform & riot shields. i raise

my spoon shove a carrot beside his small tv mouth.
i can't tell if he's eating or still begging for justice.

he waves his hands like a preacher at sunday church.
batons smile. shatter gospel & the people of ferguson

fall. cornel leaves handcuffed & hungry.
my tongue throbs losing its taste buds

& inside my mouth the carrots forget
how to compliment the corn.

A SPANISH TO ENGLISH TRANSLATION ON SWEET THINGS GONE SOUR

1. leche: milk. cream. skim milk. buttermilk. pasteurized. sour cream. half & half. half white. half privilege. privilege speaks power. colonization makes power. columbus found power. milked the land. took their cows. took their women. native american be thirsty. manifest destiny galloned all the milk. took the cookies too. forced english. this history a drought on native tongue. everybody's still thirsty. america an empty swimming pool.

2. fresa: strawberry. sweet fruit. edible red. jam. sugar blood. blood drip. bleeds on street. mike brown. hands up. cop & gun make strawberry jam on mike brown. ferguson bleeds tears. mothers' hearts bleed out. racism run savage. history repeats. too many brands of jelly. oscar grant. hands up. shoot. jam. trayvon martin. abner louimas. sean bells. jam. jelly. blood. red. too much black & red. too many emmitt till's to harvest. keep picking. fresh fruit all the time.

3. chicle: gum. tree skin. elastic sap. bad breath killer. bazooka gum. bubble tape. president's mouth bubbles bombs. feeds gum to tv throats. the people chew bubble-gum flavored: mexico not sending their best gum. criminal gum. drug dealer gum. rapists are crossing the border gum. they chew & spit gum given. not all gum lives matters. momma said chew gum with jaw closed. i never understood why gum be chewed closed. until the day i choked on bad gum.

EXPLOSIONS RIPPED THROUGH A FIREWORKS MARKET NORTH OF MEXICO CITY ON TUESDAY KILLING AT LEAST 35 PEOPLE

December 20, 2016

i see the purpose now:

for smoke/ how it billows black cloud/ to signal to god/ how sometimes god don't know/ the angel intake/or body count/ or unknown count/ or how violent life can leave/ the body/ to rename a body civilian/ death toll/ do we call this fate?/ momma would say: *si dios quiere*/ & i grew up knowing flame/ how church too burns/ to sweet smelling smoke/ that thurible of incense & charcoal we call offering/ to know wick & flame/ de veladoras/ a saint's glow is prayer/ in mexico 35 somebodies were crucible to sainthood/ at the hands of what makes fire & smoke a gorgeous couple/ a celebrated dance/ how quick a market becomes graveyard/ & a family searches out a loved one's shoe/ or bone/ as the earth shook/ as the wood charred/ as the brick fell/ & the plastic melted/ & one man told CNN en español *we have called the ambulance/ the red cross/ no one knows*/ & the smoke shadows a chapel/ i see now/ all their soot-covered faces/ splintered pews/ each lighting a candle/ & offering sky

HOW TO BE A GHOST ON EARTH

Using sections from Gloria Anzaldúa's Borderlands/La Frontera

i. definitions for ghost

███████ the supernatural ██████████████████

██████████████████████ the unknown ████████

██████ the divine ██████████ god in us ████████

██

by virtue ████████████████████████████████████

████ bleeds ████████ but does not die by virtue ████████

██████████████ is feared ██████ according to

████████████ most ████████ religion ████████████

████████████████ the █ divine ████████████████

████████████ self. ██████ is ████████████████████

████████████████████████████ Shadow ████ The

sight of her ██████████████ a frenzy of ████████ fear.

ii. definitions for ghost-mouth

█remember ████████ speaking ██████████

██ was ██████ three licks on ████████████ a

sharp ████████████████████████ corner ██████

████████████████████████ the ██████ teacher

██████████████ trying to ██████████████████

pronounce ██████████ you ██████ to be American

speak American. If you ████ like ██████████████████

where you belong.

53

SYNONYMS FOR DONALD TRUMP

1. el señor con los pelos de clote

2. trompa tonto

3. the piñata made by the people of barrio logan
   at rainbow party supplies who refuse to fill it
   with anything dulce to keep it authentic to the real thing—

   empty & hollow-hearted

TO UNDERSTAND BORDER

to understand border   is to witness your home   shrink

the size of a tangerine   be forced to split it   with a machete

     & surrender a slice   to a white man who will

harvest the meat   gnaw the pulp

grind apá's   laboring muscle   amá's   fideo de pollo

a flock of cilantro stuck   in his teeth   bittered by the salt

in our blood   guitar bones   corazónes de stone   goat heads

     & i am here: a floating moth

moon eyed   braiding back memoires   by the tattered rind

the spit seeds left   by those who take   without asking

but we too   will burst back   an orchard   knotting

our bare feet   rooted to the land

iv

NOTES ON HOW TO PULL APART THE EARTH

i. preparation

lick every meadow down to its root.
store each wild shrub behind your gums.

spoon empty the last bits of grandmother's jelly
& mason jar the night sky into your pocket.

the stars will go orphan & you will
call yourself mother & rename each luminous

point after every broken bone in your body.
tell the constellations how you heal for them.

tell the sleeping grasshoppers their wings lost purpose
to a sky of smoldering ember & the angels

have all gone home for good.

ii. dust bowl of 2030

every immigrant will grow tired
follow the wind & a nation will weep for its mother

over the outskirts the parched cows pile
like sour racks of meat buried beneath dust

here guns will grow teeth & empire the lifeless ground
replace the blooming flower

here babies will feed on chicken bones & powdered milk
our good mouths savor banquets on the pages of tattered books

let it be known the sun will contemplate its flicker
choose another lover to worship its offering heat

here rust is a merciless flood
drowns the machines made for progress

dissects the metal swallows the bolts
makes a family from bullets covered in greed

headlines will read: *everything still looks like a grave*
& mourning becomes an old habit

somewhere a ghost crawls out of a hummingbird's body
whose only song begs a country to rise

iii. a new nation

i took hair—fingerprints
forged in fire

& blacksmithed a child
bathed her in sage

tunneled our way
between a flag & fence

made to grind bodies
down to salt

built a boat from
broken crosses & cow bone

stitched the corners
in clove-hitch knots

placed a tired compass
at the bow for suggestion

found an olive tree
whose leaves hung

like bird wings
among cliffs

we claimed this refuge
wind a merciful ghost

we slept without a roof
watch each ankle buried in dust

this is how we knew warmth
in the morning i wished

my palms into bread
instead carried what

my pockets offered
the white faces of men

that led us to broken cities
i threw each coin

into the tide watched
them sink—then drown

SURVIVING THE FLOOD

listen closely you gentle shipwreck.

this is how you breathe water.

noah signed the contract. death by rain they say.

convince your lungs to play drought.

call it practice drill. teach organs to collapse.

fool the ocean. play dead. dead things are left alone.

alone means dry throat. be the wreckage turned flood

song. be sink willing light. be swollen coral & let tlaloc's

floor be home. let urchins pick the salt from your eyes

& do not panic! god promised us pearls. new vision

after the storm breaks placid. do not fight the current.

learn to be driftwood. search for sand & palm leaf.

bright. a fading mirage on this feral water & see how

the moon's reflection demands your body to survive.

LA LLORONA RETIRES THE HOLLERING
FROM HER EARS

the symphony
      she once ghosted with

now whispers

confession to the wind

strings grief
      into a pearl necklace

      sweet as her children's
      fruitful bellies

absolution is a devil tongue
      cleansed—

a scorpion's tail buds
      into flower

      blooms honey-rum pollen

& her knees crawl out the river raw

REINCARNATION

Contractors unveil 8 prototypes for Trump's border wall in San Diego
County—Tribune Media Wire
October 26, 2017

they've been out there   for weeks   metal in the sun
twisted wire   the ghost-making deed of cement   forging a dead

end   teaching a country   how to erase a country
& a people learn   to butterfly over exile

to be the swarm of bees   their pollinated backs
who learn to harpoon the wind   to march like moonlight

light-woken shadows   snake holes
the opposite to splinter   rain   like bone water

droplets of faces   offering their throats
like the neck   of the scattering dandelion

children are eager to hold

WHERE THE WILD TONGUES ARE

beyond caged teeth

    between raised fist

& shameless heart

    beasting with the wolves

standing straight for the bow

    learns to arrow

wears bullet as coat

    boiled in the blood

of motherland

    buried under snake skin

becomes brick on

    the back of resistance

beats the earth

    swallows the bees

blesses the honey

    savors the bones of bliss

CALEXICO

my city is made of people who know
the taste of sun/ on their backs
how the men & women/ can beg the earth
to be a mother/ to give birth/
to a field of harvest/ & ask its womb
again & again

how my city is a mouthful of haystack/
stray dog/ tractors/ wild canals/ how they each
dance/ against hot wind/ & blue sky
where trees break/ through drought/ & offer their
covering branches/ & we cool our throats
on raspados/ front yard sprinklers/ imaginations/ that give
us gallons of ocean/ & we bare our feet/ to the warm
ground/ to remind ourselves/ we are still children/ of the sun
how these are the tattoos/ we wear & call home

how my city knows to be a kitchen
how we invite a stranger/ to the dinner table
call them familia/ & the hands/ of brown women
labor the recipes/ from grandmothers/ to make a meal taste:
like this magic came from years:
of practice/ tired elbows/ burnt pots/ laughter/
broken hearts/ reclaimed history/ prayer

call what we make/ prayer/ maize & beans
summoned by the spices/ that have kept us alive

& yet my city too knows:/ loss/ metal fence
broke land/ broken families/ a president's insult
two-legged coyotes/ too familiar/ with thirst

how my city be made/ in god's image
& yet it too/ invites a desperate body
to know god too soon

how my city without will/ can dress itself a graveyard
& strip a child/ of its name/ how we've lost count/
see more john does/ ghosting the land/ caught
between american dreamer/ & indigenous foot step

but my city knows healing/ to be a door to a church
how we burn/ our candles/ stained glass our saints
push our rosaries/ to their fullest potential

how my city sings/ its faith with two tongues
with fresh cut marigolds/ offer pan dulce
to our loved ones/ no longer able to speak/

how we start & end/ our sentences
with:/ *si dios quiere*/ cuz if god wills it/
we are the scars/ & stories of how we chose
faith/ how after the earthquakes/ my city still
trembles/ our hips & knees/ dancing
until the sky/ grows tired

LEAVING
For Petra

the day petra left i begged the sun not to rise
but it did. clear as day the laurel leaves snapped
beneath her feet the language that spoke loudest.

she held a grocery bag. her good huaraches.
a rosary. phone numbers to el rancho. she tells me,
take this scarf hold it around your neck & remember:

the mountains. the earthworms. wet corn husk.
the stories my children exist in. i'll be right there
by the bridge tasting sunset. don't forget:

my fingers in your drying hair. rolling dough.
clay pots. the smell of zote translates te amo.
the taxi the color of spoiled milk spills over the driveway

& dissolves her body into distance. to el otro lado.
& tonight the rain drums against the rooftop.
autumn is here & i know it's your hands that keep me warm.
.

HOLDING THE NIGHT SKY

before maps— stars carried us & in blindness

we braille the sky. pluck the milky way

like white apples off its branches—

luminous freckles paving the route

to warm bread open doors honeysuckle—

how even the dim-eyed beetle holds the night

responsible to candle its footsteps home.

how we've forgotten the furthest of fires that gave

name to stones the size of wolves—

gave wolves reason to bloom song. to remind

the earth the sun will rise & burn.

PRAYER

sometimes prayer appears in the shape of six mexicans in a bedroom. we squeeze rosary beads & wish a pomegranate to bloom from our hands into our mouths. instead momma says every decade shoots through the popcorn ceiling. cuts through the clouds. knocks at la virgen or baby jesus or whoever clocks in that day to transcribe a *hail mary & our father*—to resurrect a mother's dead child. provide a safe path across a grave-offering desert & i imagine prayer works like this: a saint picks momma's prayer from a jar like a seed & momma prays for tia irma's cancer. for dad's stiff joints. for the dying dog at the border. she says *don't forget to say your amens or jesusito won't hear us.* amen. amen. amen & in the palm of a glowing saint a seed demands to be a garden.

GATHERING THE FRAGMENTS
After Tracey K. Smith

after darkness

we'll swallow the light

become the stars that left

us to beckon the matchbox

gather the pieces

bend & curve their edges

pull the sky over rust

un-fossil families out of hiding

having outlived every threat

we'll plant a fig tree

for every life lost

our memories the medicine

to rebuild ourselves

back to good blood hard bone

we'll chip away at what pushed

us back: dictators molasses roads black noise

our homes will be built of books

written from the faces of those

who sacrificed their sharp mouths

to keep us here

NOTES

BISABUELA MARRIED A SPANIARD
•In the poem "Bisabuela Married a Spaniard" is dedicated to my great grandmother Maria Luisa Medellin who was part of the Chichimeca peoples. Medellin married my great grandfather, Rafael Cordero, a Spaniard who settled in Matehuala, San Luis Potosí. They married in 1951.

HISTORY OF WALLS
•The line, "my home rhymes with mexico & ends with a wall." is in reference to my hometown, Calexico, CA and the border that runs along the land.

TENOCHTITLAN
• "Tenochtitlan" is a term that references the capital of the Aztec empire founded in Lake Texcoco, c. 1325. Located now in modern Mexico City, the ancient prophecy of Tenochtitlan was founded by a tribe who witnessed an eagle with a snake perched on a prickly pair cactus (Opuntia).

HIJA DE LA COSECHA
• "Hija de la Cosecha" is Spanish for "daughter of harvest."

IN A DREAM A SMALL STATUE OF LA VIRGEN DE GUADALUPE PREPARES TO DIVE FROM THE BOOKSHELF
• La Virgen de Guadalupe is in reference to "Our Lady of Guadalupe," "Mother of God," "Nahua goddess Tonantzin."

TRUTHS AT THE ALL-AMERICAN CANAL
•The "All-American Canal" is an 80 mile long aqueduct in Southern California which carries water from the Colorado river into the Imperial Valley. According to CBS News: 60 Minutes, over 550 people have drowned in the All-American Canal, this number includes undocumented immigrants.

FALSE SECURITY: A STORY TOLD FROM EVE'S RIBCAGE
•False Security: A story told from Eve's Ribcage is a poem created in collaboration with Hari Alluri. The invented form called "ribcage" is presented in a six-syllable count on each side of the ribcage.

PARTS & DEFINITIONS FOR MESTIZA-MOUTH
• According to Gloria Anzaldúa's text, Borderlands/La Frontera: The New Mestiza, the term Mestiza is defined as "una nueva raza, el mestizo, el mexicano (people of mixed Indian and Spanish blood)."

HOW TO BE A GHOST ON EARTH

•In the poem, "How To Be A Ghost On Earth" is an erasure poem based from Gloria Anzaldúa's text, *Borderlands/La Frontera: The New Mestiza*. Part I. Definitions for ghost, borrows texts from Chapter 2 'Movimientos de rebeldía y las culturas que traicionana' page 25. Part II. Definitions for ghost, borrows text from Chapter 5 'How to tame a wild tongue' page 75.

SURVIVING THE FLOOD

•In the poem "Surviving the Flood" is a poem in response to sam sax's poem "Learning to Breathe Water." In addition the term "Tlaloc" is a term for the god of rain within Aztec religion.

ACKNOWLEDGEMENTS

Thank you to the editors of the following journals and anthologies, who published these poems in their original or early stages of their birth:

The Acentos Review: "A Brown Girl's Blues"

ANMLY: "Bisabuela Married a Spaniard" and "How To Be a Ghost on Earth"

Bettering American Poetry (Bettering Books): "his jawbone caged my grandfather's skin"

The Blue Shift Journal- The Speak Easy Project: "La Llorona Retires the Hollering From Her Ears"

BOAAT Press: "Reincarnation"

The Boiler: "Hija de la Cosecha" and "Deity"

Button Poetry: "The Time Momma Gave Me The Chancla For Letting Andrew Jackson Escape Out The Window"

Cosmonauts Avenue Poetry: "I once cracked open the earth" and "Christmas"

Dialogue- A Publication of the San Diego Area Writing Project: "don't be afraid to speak" and "why the hand labors an alphabet"

FreezeRay: "The first time I met the KKK" and "Chicana Learns Survival From the Teenage Mutant Ninja Turtles"

Heart Journal Online: "I watch all the drought thirsty things the desert carries," "Leaving," "Arrival," and "To Understand Border"

Imaniman: Poets Writing in the Anzaldúan Borderlands (Aunt Lute Books): "Where The Wilds Tongues Are"

Nailed Magazine: "Bean Mythology," "Zoo of Eden," "A Spanish To English Translation of Sour Things Gone Sour," and "A Lesson in Sowing"

Latinas: Struggles and Protests in 21 st Century USA (Red Sugarcane Press): "A History of Walls"

PANK Magazine: "Where I Inherit My Silence" and " Leaked Audio From A Detention Center"

Read America(s): An Anthology (Locked Horn Press): "El Rancho 92'" and "this skin be"

Tinderbox Poetry: "his jawbone caged my grandfather's skin," "a history of walls," and "Watching The Green Mile For The First Time & I Dream That Night Knowing John Coffey Could Have Also Been My Father"

Track//Four Journal: "Prayer to Mexico" and "The Time Momma Gave Me The Chancla For Letting Andrew Jackson Escape Out The Window"

Souvenir: "My city is panting"

Words Dance Publishing: "My momma knows all the monsters' hidden teeth" and "Abuela is a machete wrapped in her favorite apron"

My deepest gratitude to the folks who've given this book and poet the lungs necessary to create fearlessly:

To my family: my mother a.k.a. Big Momma, Dad a.k.a Heli Jackson, thank you for your love and work ethic. To Alfonso Cordero, thank you for your stories. To the ancestors. To my hermanas: Karina, Kassandra, and Kathia. To the Cordero Family and DeMatteo Family in supporting all of my endeavors.

To my trusting editors: my partner in crime and love, Mario DeMatteo and Alfredo Aguilar a.k.a El Niño. I write because of your support, feedback, talent, and persistence. Thank you!

To Alfonso Wong, Cenit Wong, Chase Pamplin, Garik Pugh for directing, shooting, and editing videos for poems in this collection.

To my familia beyond blood:
SDSU MFA squad. To my fairy god poetry parents: Ilya Kaminsky, Sherwin Bitsui, Piotr Florczyk, Sandra Alcosser, Marilyn Chin, Jenny Minniti-Shippey, Sarah B. Marsh-Rebelo, Mary Garcia, Hari Alluri, Phillip Serrato. The many professors in the Literature and Rhetoric Department at SDSU.

Glassless Minds, Pink Door 2015, Rachel McKibbens, Stevie Edwards, Cynthia Dewi Oka, The Loft Literary Center, Bao Phi, Elevated Slam Team 2013: Ant Black, Joe Limer, Jerrica Escoto, Preston Ronald Clark, Christopher Wilson, San Diego Poetry and Los Angeles Poetry Community (DPL poets), Yesika Salgado, Edwin Bodney, Aziza Barnes.

VONA Familia 2018: Elle Bosque, Ana Diaz, Leo Simonovis, pinche Angelina Sáenz, Gabriel Cortez, Sergio Lima, Irene Sanchez. Shout out to Willie Perdomo thank you for your wisdom.

Macondo Familia 2018: Melissa Bennett, Xochit-Julisa Bermejo, Antonio Lopez, Cecilia Macias-McCardle, Juan J. Morales, Gerardo Pacheco, Willy Palomo, Angela Penaredoñdo, Sabrina San Miguel, Natalia Treviño. My love to Allison Adelle Hedge Coke for reminding me to always say rooted.

San Diego Area Writing Project 2017 Crew, the SDAWP Writing Familia: Christine Kane, Mia Faulk, Denise Maduli-Williams.

Thank you to Maria Figueroa for your mentorship. Thank you to the amazing support system at MiraCosta College and San Diego City College, for giving me the balance to be both educator and artist.

Thank you all for your influences, motivation, encouragement, and support. I'm endlessly grateful!

Thank you to the artists behind the scenes in making this book possible: to my editor Safia Elhillo, book cover artist Juan Charlie Beaz, book designer Ian DeLucca and Mario DeMatteo and to the press that believed in this book Not a Cult. and founder Daniel Lisi, thank you!

To Petra, thank you for your motherhood, for being my otro lado, you will forever be remembered.

To Calexico, my city that gave me the roots to grow.

To you reader, thank you for holding this book, for giving this collection the legs to run.

ABOUT THE AUTHOR

Kathia Cordero

Karla Cordero is a descendant of the Chichimeca people from Northern Mexico, born and raised along the borderlands of Calexico, CA. She is a Macondo, VONA, CantoMundo, and Pink Door Retreat fellow, a recipient of The Loft Spoken Word Immersion Fellowship, and the San Diego State University Global Diversity Award. Her work has appeared in journals and anthologies including *PANK, BOAAT, Anomaly, Imaniman: Poets Writing in the Anzaldúan Borderlands,* and *Bettering American Poetry.* She is the author of the chapbook, *Grasshoppers Before Gods* (Dancing Girl Press 2016), founder of *Voice 4 Change* Reading Series, and editor of *Spit Journal.* Karla currently serves as an associate professor of English and Creative Writing at MiraCosta and San Diego City College.

You can find out more about her at
www.karlacordero.com

🅕 🅞 🅨 🅞

For events and catalog information:
notacult.media

Not a Cult's Fall 2019 catalog

Hermosa by Yesika Salgado
ISBN 978-1-945649-33-2

the blind pig by Aziza Barnes
ISBN 978-1-945649-32-5

From Rufio to Zuko by Dante Basco
Lost Boys Edition ISBN 978-1-945649-35-6
Fire Nation Edition ISBN 978-1-945649-36-3

Books distributed by SCB Distributors